SPEND LESS AND GET MORE: HOLIDAY GUIDE

Olivia Frugal

North Bees LLC

Published by North Bees LLC

To those who believe in the magic of the season but understand the beauty of mindful spending, to the thrifty celebrators who turn ordinary moments into extraordinary memories, and to all who know that joy need not come with a hefty price tag,

This book is dedicated to you, the architects of budget-friendly celebrations and the maestros of making every penny count. May the pages of "Spend Less and Get More: Holiday Guide" be your compass to a holiday season filled with warmth, laughter, and the priceless joy that comes from clever, frugal festivities.

With festive cheer and financial wisdom,

Olivia Frugal

CONTENTS

Title Page

Copyright

Dedication

Foreword

Chapter 1 : Introduction   1

Chapter 2 : Creating a Holiday Budget   8

Chapter 3 : Smart Shopping Strategies   15

Chapter 4 : DIY Gifts and Decorations   18

Chapter 5 : Maximizing Your Savings   24

Chapter 6 : Alternative Gift-Giving   33

Chapter 7 : Managing Holiday Travel Expenses   39

Chapter 8 : Hosting on a Budget   44

Chapter 9 : Avoiding Post-Holiday Debt   53

Chapter 10 : Embracing the True Spirit of the Holidays   65

Afterword   73

About The Author   75

FOREWORD

Welcome to "Spend Less and Get More: Holiday Guide," where the magic of the holidays meets the art of frugality. In these pages, Olivia Frugal, our anonymous guide, invites you to reimagine your celebrations without sacrificing the joy that makes the season special.

This guide is not just about saving money; it's a roadmap to creating meaningful moments that linger in your heart long after the tinsel is stored away. Olivia's insights are a testament to the belief that holiday magic doesn't have to come with a hefty price tag. As you embark on this frugal festive journey, may you discover that the most precious gifts are often the simplest, and that joy can be found in the thoughtful details of each celebration.

Here's to a holiday season filled with abundance, creativity, and the satisfaction of spending less while getting more.

CHAPTER 1 :
INTRODUCTION

*Setting the Stage for a Joyful and
Budget-Friendly Holiday Season*

Welcome to 'Spend Less and Get More: Your Ultimate Holiday Guide,' where we embark on a journey to transform your holidays into unforgettable experiences without breaking the bank. In this chapter, we will set the stage by highlighting the importance of budgeting during the holidays, understanding the psychological aspects of consumerism, and identifying common holiday spending traps.

The holiday season is a time of joy, love, and celebration. It's a time when we come together with our loved ones to create lasting memories and express gratitude. However, amidst the cheer and merriment, there often lurks a cloud of financial stress. The pressure to spend extravagantly on gifts, decorations, travel, and hosting can quickly drain our bank accounts and leave us with post-holiday debt.

That's why budgeting during the holidays is not just a good idea; it's an essential tool for maintaining financial well-being and ensuring a stress-free and fulfilling holiday season. By setting a budget and sticking to it, we can make intentional choices about where to allocate our resources and focus on what truly matters: creating meaningful experiences with our loved ones.

But why is it so important to understand the psychological aspects of consumerism during the holidays? Well, the holiday season has become synonymous with shopping and gift-giving. Advertisements bombard us with messages that convince us we need to buy the latest gadgets, trendy clothes, and extravagant presents to show our love and appreciation. It's easy to get caught up in the frenzy of consumerism and lose sight of what the holidays are truly about.

In this chapter, we will delve into the psychological tricks that marketers use to influence our spending habits during the holidays. By understanding these tactics, we can become more aware consumers and make informed decisions that align with our values and priorities.

Additionally, we will explore common holiday spending traps that many people fall into year after year. From impulse buying to succumbing to the pressure of keeping up with societal expectations, we will uncover the pitfalls that can derail our budgeting efforts. By recognizing these traps, we can navigate the holiday season with confidence and avoid unnecessary financial stress.

So, get ready to embark on this budgeting journey with us. Together, we will discover the secrets to a joyful and budget-friendly holiday season. Let's take control of our finances, create unforgettable memories, and embrace the true spirit of the holidays. Welcome to 'Spend Less and Get More: Your Ultimate Holiday Guide.'

Setting the Stage: The Importance of Budgeting During the Holidays

The holiday season is a time of joy, excitement, and celebration. It's a time when we gather with loved ones, exchange gifts, and create lasting memories. However, amidst all the merriment, it's easy to get caught up in the frenzy of holiday expenses and overspend without even realizing it. This is why setting a budget during the holidays is of utmost importance.

1.1 The True Meaning of the Holidays

Before delving into the specifics of budgeting, it's crucial to remind ourselves of the true meaning of the holidays. The holiday season is not about how much money we spend or the lavishness of our celebrations. It's about cherishing our relationships, expressing gratitude, and finding joy in the simplest of things. By keeping this in mind, we can shift our focus from materialistic desires to creating meaningful experiences.

1.2 The Psychological Aspects of Consumerism

Consumerism plays a significant role during the holiday season. Advertisements bombard us with messages that make us feel like we need to buy more to experience happiness and fulfillment. This constant pressure to spend can lead to impulse buying and overspending. Understanding the psychological aspects of consumerism can help us make more mindful choices and resist the temptation to succumb to unnecessary purchases.

1.3 Identifying Common Holiday Spending Traps

To effectively budget during the holidays, we need to be aware of the common spending traps that can derail our financial plans. One of the most common traps is the allure of holiday sales and discounts. Retailers often offer attractive deals and promotions, making it easy for us to justify unnecessary purchases. Another trap is the pressure to keep up with societal expectations. We may feel compelled to buy expensive gifts or host extravagant parties to meet perceived standards. By identifying these traps, we can proactively avoid them and make informed decisions about our spending.

1.4 The Benefits of Budgeting

Now that we understand the importance of budgeting during the holidays, let's explore the benefits it brings. Firstly, budgeting allows us to take control of our finances and set realistic spending limits. It helps us prioritize our expenses and allocate funds to what truly matters to us. Budgeting also helps reduce stress and anxiety associated with overspending. By having a clear plan in place, we can enjoy the holiday season without constantly worrying about our finances. Moreover, budgeting encourages us to be more creative and thoughtful in our gift-giving and celebrations. When we have limited resources, we are forced to think outside the box and find meaningful ways to express our love and appreciation.

In the following subsections, we will delve deeper into each of these aspects and provide practical tips and strategies to help you create a budget that allows you to spend less and get more out of the holiday season.

The Psychology of Consumerism: Understanding Holiday Spending Traps

The holiday season is a time of joy, love, and celebration. It's a time when we come together with our loved ones, exchange gifts, and create beautiful memories. However, it's also a time when we can easily fall into the trap of consumerism. Understanding the psychological aspects of consumerism is crucial to avoid overspending and financial stress during the holidays.

Subsection 1: The Emotional Appeal of Holiday Advertising

During the holiday season, we are bombarded with advertisements that play on our emotions. Advertisers are experts at creating a sense of urgency, making us feel like we have to buy certain products or risk missing out on the perfect gift. They use emotional triggers such as family, love, and happiness to persuade us to open our wallets. It's essential to recognize these tactics and not let them dictate our spending habits.

Subsection 2: The Fear of Missing Out (FOMO)

One of the most common traps during the holiday season is the fear of missing out (FOMO). We see our friends and family buying extravagant gifts, hosting lavish parties, and going on luxurious vacations. It's easy to compare ourselves to others and feel the pressure to keep up. But it's important to remember that everyone's financial situation is different, and trying to match someone else's spending can lead to financial strain.

Subsection 3: The Power of Social Proof

Social proof is a powerful psychological phenomenon that influences our behavior. When we see others buying certain products or following specific trends, it creates a sense of validation and makes us more likely to do the same. During the holiday season, social media platforms are flooded with posts showcasing extravagant gifts and holiday experiences. It's crucial to remember that what we see online is often a curated version of reality, and we shouldn't base our own spending decisions solely on what others are doing.

Subsection 4: The Instant Gratification Trap

Consumerism thrives on the desire for instant gratification. We want to experience joy and happiness immediately, and buying things seems to offer a quick fix. However, this instant gratification comes at a cost. Overspending during the holidays can lead to financial stress and debt that will linger long after the decorations are put away. It's important to be mindful of the long-term consequences of impulsive spending.

Subsection 5: The Power of Marketing Techniques

Marketers employ various techniques to influence our buying decisions. From limited-time offers and flash sales to free shipping and discounts, these tactics are designed to create a sense of urgency and make us feel like we're getting a great deal. However, it's essential to take a step back and evaluate whether we truly need the item or if we're simply falling for the marketing hype.

Subsection 6: The Influence of Childhood Memories

Our childhood memories play a significant role in shaping our holiday traditions and spending habits. Many of us have nostalgic associations with specific products or experiences during the holidays. Advertisers capitalize on these emotions by using familiar jingles, images, and characters that evoke feelings of warmth and nostalgia. By understanding the influence of childhood memories, we can make more conscious choices about our holiday spending.

Subsection 7: The Role of Peer Pressure

Peer pressure is not limited to teenagers; it can also affect our spending habits as adults. We may feel pressured to buy expensive gifts or host elaborate parties to impress our friends, family, and colleagues. However, it's important to prioritize our financial well-being over societal expectations. True friends and loved ones will appreciate the thought and effort behind a meaningful gift, regardless of its price tag.

Conclusion:

By understanding the psychology behind consumerism, we can make more informed decisions and avoid falling into the holiday spending traps. It's essential to be aware of the emotional appeal of advertising, the fear of missing out, the power of social proof, the instant gratification trap, marketing techniques, the influence of childhood memories, and the role of peer pressure. By staying mindful of these factors, we can create a holiday season that is joyful, meaningful, and financially responsible.

Conclusion

In this chapter, we discussed the importance of budgeting during the holidays and the psychological aspects of consumerism that often influence our spending habits. We also identified common holiday spending traps that can derail our financial plans. As we move forward in this book, it's essential to remember that spending less and getting more is not just about saving money; it's about making deliberate choices that align with our values and priorities. Here are some key takeaways and actionable advice to keep in mind:

1. Create a realistic holiday budget: Take the time to assess your financial situation and set a budget that reflects your income and expenses. Be mindful of your spending limits and prioritize your expenses accordingly.

2. Understand your motivations: Recognize the psychological factors that drive consumerism and be aware of the emotional triggers that may lead to impulse buying. Practice mindfulness and question whether a purchase aligns with your true needs and desires.

3. Avoid common spending traps: Stay vigilant of common holiday spending traps, such as sales and discounts that encourage overspending, peer pressure to buy extravagant gifts, and the temptation to keep up with others' expectations. Be intentional about your purchases and resist the pressure to spend beyond your means.

By applying these principles and strategies, you can find joy in the holiday season without compromising your financial well-being. In the next chapter, we will explore practical tips and strategies to help you plan and execute a budget-friendly holiday season.

CHAPTER 2 : CREATING A HOLIDAY BUDGET

Creating a Holiday Budget: Your Key to a Stress-Free and Financially Responsible Holiday Season

Welcome to Chapter 2 of 'Spend Less and Get More: Your Ultimate Holiday Guide.' In this chapter, we will delve into the essential topic of creating a holiday budget. As you embark on your journey towards a joyful and budget-friendly holiday season, it is crucial to lay a solid foundation for your financial decisions. By setting realistic spending limits and tracking your expenses, you can ensure that you stay on track and avoid unnecessary financial stress.

Assessing your financial situation is the first step towards creating a holiday budget that works for you. Take a moment to reflect on your current financial standing and determine how much you can comfortably allocate towards holiday expenses. Consider your income, savings, and any outstanding debts or financial commitments. By understanding your financial limitations, you can make informed decisions and avoid overspending.

Once you have a clear picture of your financial situation, it's time to set realistic spending limits. Determine how much you can afford to spend on different aspects of the holiday season, such as gifts, decorations, food, and travel. Be honest with yourself and prioritize your expenses based on what truly matters to you and your loved ones. Remember, the key is to strike a balance between celebrating and staying within your means.

Tracking and managing expenses is essential to stay on top of your holiday budget. Keep a record of every expense, no matter how small, and categorize them accordingly. This will help you identify any areas where you may be overspending and allow you to make adjustments as needed. Utilize budgeting tools or apps that can assist you in tracking your expenses effortlessly.

Creating a holiday budget may seem like a tedious task, but it is a vital step towards a stress-free and financially responsible holiday season. By taking the time to assess your financial situation, set realistic spending limits, and track your expenses, you will gain control over your finances and ensure that you make the most of your holiday celebrations.

In the upcoming sections of this chapter, we will explore each of these points in detail, providing you with practical tips and strategies to create a holiday budget that works for you. Get ready to take charge of your finances and make this holiday season truly unforgettable!

Assessing Your Financial Situation: The Key to Creating a Holiday Budget

The holiday season is a time of joy, celebration, and giving. It's also a time when many people find themselves overspending and facing financial stress in the aftermath. One of the most effective ways to avoid this holiday budget trap is by assessing your financial situation and creating a realistic spending plan. In this section, we will explore the importance of assessing your financial situation and provide you with practical tips to create a holiday budget that works for you.

Subsection 1: Taking Stock of Your Finances

Before diving into the world of holiday budgeting, it's crucial to take a step back and assess your current financial situation. Start by gathering all your financial documents, including bank statements, credit card bills, and any other relevant information. Take a close look at your income, expenses, and outstanding debts. This will give you a clear picture of your financial health and help you determine how much you can afford to spend during the holiday season.

Subsection 2: Setting Realistic Spending Limits

Once you have a clear understanding of your financial situation, it's time to set realistic spending limits for the holiday season. Take into account your income, monthly expenses, and any upcoming financial obligations. Consider how much you can comfortably allocate towards holiday-related expenses without compromising your financial stability.

Subsection 3: Prioritizing Holiday Expenses

Creating a holiday budget involves making choices and prioritizing your spending. It's essential to identify the expenses that matter most to you and allocate funds accordingly. For example, if spending quality time with loved ones is your top priority, allocate a larger portion of your budget towards travel or hosting expenses. If you enjoy giving gifts, allocate a portion of your budget towards thoughtful presents for your loved ones. By prioritizing your expenses, you can allocate your resources wisely and avoid overspending.

Subsection 4: Tracking and Managing Expenses

To stay on track with your holiday budget, it's important to track and manage your expenses. Start by keeping a record of all your holiday-related spending, including gifts, decorations, food, and travel expenses. Use a spreadsheet, budgeting app, or a simple pen and paper to jot down every expense. Regularly review your spending to ensure that you're staying within your budget. If you find that you're exceeding your spending limits in one area, look for opportunities to cut back in another.

Subsection 5: Adjusting Your Budget as Needed

Creating a holiday budget is not a one-time task. It's an ongoing process that requires flexibility and adjustment. As the holiday season progresses, you may encounter unexpected expenses or changes in your financial situation. Be prepared to adapt and modify your budget as needed. Regularly assess your progress and make necessary adjustments to ensure that you're staying on track.

By assessing your financial situation and creating a holiday budget that aligns with your financial goals, you can enjoy a stress-free and fulfilling holiday season without breaking the bank. Remember, the key is to be realistic, prioritize your expenses, and track your spending. With these strategies in place, you'll be well on your way to spending less and getting more this holiday season.

Tracking and Managing Expenses

Tracking and managing your expenses during the holiday season is crucial to staying within your budget and avoiding any post-holiday financial stress. In this section, we will explore effective strategies to help you keep a close eye on your spending and make necessary adjustments along the way. Let's dive in!

Subsection 1: Establishing a Holiday Expense Tracker

To effectively track your holiday expenses, it's essential to establish a comprehensive expense tracker. This can be done either using a spreadsheet on your computer or a mobile app specifically designed for expense tracking. Here are some key steps to get you started:

1. Categorize Your Expenses: Begin by creating categories for different types of holiday expenses such as gifts, decorations, food, travel, and entertainment. This will help you organize your spending and identify areas where you can potentially cut back.

2. Set Spending Limits: Assign a specific spending limit for each category based on your budget. This will help you prioritize your expenses and avoid overspending in any particular area.

3. Record Every Expense: Make it a habit to record every holiday-related expense, no matter how small. Include details like date, item or service purchased, cost, and the category it falls under. This level of detail will give you a clear picture of your spending patterns.

4. Regularly Update Your Tracker: Dedicate some time each day or at least once a week to update your expense tracker. This will ensure that you have an accurate and up-to-date view of your spending throughout the holiday season.

Subsection 2: Analyzing and Adjusting Your Budget

Once you have a system in place for tracking your expenses, the next step is to analyze your spending patterns and make necessary adjustments to stay on track with your budget. Here's how you can do it:

1. Review Your Tracker Regularly: Take some time each week to review your expense tracker and compare your actual spending with your budgeted amounts. This will help you identify any areas where you might be overspending and make adjustments accordingly.

2. Identify Areas for Cost Reduction: Look for opportunities to cut costs without sacrificing the joy of the holiday season. For example, you might find that you're spending more on decorations than you initially planned. In such cases, consider DIY options or explore affordable alternatives.

3. Prioritize Your Spending: If you find that you're exceeding your budget in certain categories, prioritize your spending by focusing on the most important items or experiences. This way, you can allocate your resources wisely and still enjoy the holiday season without overspending.

4. Seek Ways to Save: Keep an eye out for discounts, coupons, and special offers that can help you save money on holiday purchases. Look for sales, compare prices, and consider shopping online to find the best deals.

Subsection 3: Staying Disciplined and Avoiding Impulse Purchases

One of the biggest challenges during the holiday season is resisting the temptation of impulse purchases. Here are some tips to help you stay disciplined:

1. Stick to Your Shopping List: Before heading out to shop, create a detailed shopping list that includes everything you need. Stick to this list and avoid making unplanned purchases.

2. Take Advantage of Sales: While it's important to stick to your list, it's also wise to take advantage of sales and discounts on items that you had planned to purchase. Just be sure that the sale price aligns with your budget and the item is something you genuinely need.

3. Avoid Emotional Spending: It's easy to get caught up in the holiday spirit and make impulsive purchases based on emotions rather than rational thinking. Before making any purchase, take a moment to consider if it aligns with your budget and if it's something you truly need or want.

4. Practice Delayed Gratification: If you come across an item that you're tempted to buy but it's not on your list, give yourself some time to think it over. Delayed gratification can help you make more informed decisions and avoid buyer's remorse.

By following these steps, you'll be able to enjoy the holiday season without the stress of overspending. Creating a solid holiday budget allows you to make thoughtful and intentional choices, ensuring that your celebrations are filled with joy and financial peace of mind. Happy budgeting!

CHAPTER 3 :
SMART SHOPPING
STRATEGIES

Welcome to Chapter 3 of 'Spend Less and Get More: Your Ultimate Holiday Guide.' In this chapter, we will dive into the world of smart shopping strategies, where we will unravel the secrets to saving money and getting the most out of your holiday purchases.

Mastering the Art of Smart Shopping

In today's fast-paced consumer culture, it's easy to get caught up in the excitement of shopping and overspend on items you don't really need. But with some smart shopping strategies, you can save money and make the most of your holiday budget. In this section, we will explore several effective techniques to help you become a savvy shopper and get the most bang for your buck.

Researching and Comparing Prices:

When it comes to holiday shopping, knowledge is power. Before making any purchase, take the time to research and compare prices. This simple step can save you a significant amount of money. Start by browsing online marketplaces, retail websites, and local stores to get an idea of the average price range for the items on your shopping list. Take note of any ongoing promotions or discounts that may be available.

Once you have an idea of the general price range, it's time to compare prices. Visit multiple stores or websites that offer the same product and compare their prices. Keep an eye out for sales, clearance items, or special holiday promotions. Don't forget to consider additional costs such as shipping fees or taxes when comparing prices.

Making Use of Coupons, Discounts, and Loyalty Programs:

Coupons, discounts, and loyalty programs can be your best friends during the holiday season. They offer great opportunities to save money on your purchases. Start by searching for coupons online or in local newspapers. Many retailers also offer discounts or exclusive promotions to their loyal customers. Sign up for loyalty programs and take advantage of the benefits they offer, such as early access to sales or exclusive discounts.

When using coupons or discounts, make sure to read the fine print and understand any limitations or restrictions. Some coupons may have expiration dates, minimum purchase requirements, or specific conditions for use. Always double-check the terms and conditions to ensure you are getting the maximum benefit.

Avoiding Impulse Buying and Sticking to Your Shopping List:

Impulse buying can quickly derail your holiday budget. To avoid falling into this trap, make a shopping list before heading out to the stores or browsing online. Write down the items you need and prioritize them based on importance. Be specific about the features or specifications you are looking for in each item.

Once you have your shopping list, stick to it. Avoid getting swayed by attractive displays, flashy promotions, or last-minute deals that are not on your list. Stay focused on your priorities and remind yourself of your budget limitations. If you come across an item that is not on your list but catches your attention, take a moment to evaluate whether it is a necessary purchase or simply an impulse buy.

By following these smart shopping strategies, you can make the most of your holiday budget and ensure that you get the best value for your money. Researching and comparing prices, making use of coupons, discounts, and loyalty programs, and avoiding impulse buying will help you stay on track and achieve a joyful and budget-friendly holiday season. Happy shopping!

To summarize, the key takeaways from this chapter are:

1. Research and compare prices before making a purchase to ensure you get the best deal.

2. Utilize coupons, discounts, and loyalty programs to save even more money.

3. Resist the temptation of impulse buying by sticking to your shopping list.

By following these smart shopping strategies, you can make the most of your holiday shopping and achieve a balance between saving money and getting the things you need. Happy shopping and enjoy the savings!

CHAPTER 4 : DIY GIFTS AND DECORATIONS

Welcome to Chapter 4 of 'Spend Less and Get More: Your Ultimate Holiday Guide.' In this chapter, we dive into the exciting world of do-it-yourself (DIY) gifts and decorations, where creativity meets affordability. Are you tired of giving generic store-bought gifts that lack personal touch? Do you dream of transforming your home into a cozy and festive wonderland without breaking the bank? Look no further! In this chapter, we will explore a plethora of creative and affordable homemade gift ideas that will delight your loved ones and make a lasting impression.

The Art of Homemade Gifts: Expressing Love and Creativity

The holiday season is a time of giving, and what better way to show your love and appreciation than by gifting something handmade? Homemade gifts hold a special place in the hearts of both the giver and the recipient. They are not only budget-friendly but also carry a personal touch that store-bought presents often lack. In this section, we will explore a variety of creative and affordable homemade gift ideas that will leave a lasting impression on your loved ones.

Subsection 1: Handcrafted Jewelry

Jewelry has always been a timeless and cherished gift. Instead of purchasing expensive pieces, why not try your hand at making your own? With a little creativity and some basic materials, you can create stunning pieces that are unique and meaningful. Consider making beaded bracelets or necklaces using colorful beads and charms. Experiment with different designs and patterns to match the recipient's style and personality. Not only will you save money, but you'll also be able to customize each piece to make it truly special.

Subsection 2: Personalized Photo Albums

Photos capture precious moments and memories that we hold dear. Transform these cherished memories into beautiful personalized photo albums. Gather your favorite pictures and create a storybook-like album using scrapbooking materials. Add captions, stickers, and decorative elements to make each page come alive. You can even include handwritten notes and messages to make it even more personal. This heartfelt gift will not only bring back fond memories but also serve as a keepsake that can be treasured for years to come.

Subsection 3: Homemade Candles

Candles add warmth and ambiance to any space, making them a popular choice for gifts. Instead of buying expensive candles from stores, why not make your own scented creations? All you need are some wax flakes, essential oils, wicks, and containers. Melt the wax, add your chosen fragrance, and pour it into the containers. You can get creative with different colors and shapes, or even add dried flowers or herbs for a unique touch. Not only will you save money, but you'll also have the satisfaction of knowing that you created something beautiful and fragrant.

Subsection 4: Hand-knit Scarves

Winter is the perfect time to cozy up with warm accessories, and what better gift than a beautifully hand-knit scarf? Knitting may seem intimidating, but it's a skill that can be easily learned with practice. Choose soft and cozy yarn in the recipient's favorite colors, and start knitting away. You can experiment with different patterns and stitches to create a unique design. The effort and love put into each stitch will be evident in the final product, making it a truly special gift.

Subsection 5: Customized Recipe Books

Food brings people together, and a customized recipe book filled with family favorites and secret recipes is a gift that will be cherished for generations. Collect your family's treasured recipes and compile them into a beautifully designed book. Include personal anecdotes, cooking tips, and photos to make it even more special. This gift not only celebrates the joy of cooking but also preserves family traditions and creates a lasting legacy.

Subsection 6: Homemade Spa Kits

Pamper your loved ones with luxurious homemade spa kits. Gather a selection of natural ingredients such as bath salts, essential oils, body scrubs, and face masks. Package them in attractive containers and include a set of instructions for each product. You can even customize the scents and ingredients based on the recipient's preferences. This thoughtful gift will allow them to relax and unwind in the comfort of their own home.

By exploring these creative and affordable homemade gift ideas, you can not only save money but also create heartfelt presents that will be cherished for years to come. The joy and satisfaction of giving something handmade are immeasurable, and your loved ones will appreciate the time and effort you put into each gift. So embrace your creativity, involve your family and friends in the process, and let the joy of DIY gift-giving make this holiday season truly special.

Creative and Affordable Homemade Gift Ideas

Creating homemade gifts is not only a budget-friendly option but also adds a personal touch to your holiday presents. In this section, we will explore a variety of creative and affordable homemade gift ideas that will surely impress your loved ones. From handmade crafts to delicious treats, these gifts are not only thoughtful but also fun to make. Let's dive right in!

Subsection 1: Handmade Crafts

Handmade crafts are a wonderful way to show your creativity and create unique gifts that will be cherished by the recipients. Here are a few ideas to get you started:

1. DIY Photo Frame: Personalize a plain photo frame by decorating it with paint, glitter, or other embellishments. Insert a photo of a special memory with the recipient to make it even more meaningful.

2. Customized Tote Bag: Purchase a plain canvas tote bag and use fabric paint or markers to create a custom design. You can add the recipient's name, favorite quote, or a fun pattern that reflects their personality.

3. Hand-Stamped Jewelry: Create one-of-a-kind jewelry pieces by stamping meaningful words or symbols onto metal blanks. Necklaces, bracelets, and keychains are all great options. You can also add birthstones or charms to make it even more special.

Subsection 2: Delicious Treats

Who doesn't love receiving homemade treats during the holiday season? From cookies to jams, there are endless possibilities for delicious edible gifts. Here are a few ideas:

1. Holiday Cookies: Bake a variety of festive cookies, such as gingerbread, sugar cookies, or peppermint chocolate chip cookies. Package them in decorative tins or mason jars and add a personalized tag.

2. Homemade Fudge: Whip up a batch of creamy fudge in flavors like chocolate, peanut butter, or salted caramel. Cut them into

bite-sized pieces and package them in festive gift boxes or bags.

3. Infused Oils and Vinegars: Create flavored oils and vinegars by infusing them with herbs, spices, or fruits. Pour them into decorative bottles and attach recipe cards with suggested uses.

Subsection 3: Personalized Gifts

Personalized gifts are always a hit because they show that you've put thought and effort into creating something unique for the recipient. Here are a few ideas:

1. Customized Photo Calendar: Use online services or software to create a personalized photo calendar featuring pictures of the recipient's loved ones, special events, or memorable moments.

2. Monogrammed Items: Personalize items like towels, mugs, or tote bags with the recipient's initials. You can use fabric markers, embroidery, or vinyl decals.

3. Memory Jar: Decorate a glass jar and fill it with handwritten notes or small trinkets that represent special memories you've shared with the recipient. They can pull out a memory whenever they need a pick-me-up.

Subsection 4: DIY Gift Kits

Gift kits are a great way to provide everything needed for a specific activity or hobby. Here are a few ideas:

1. Spa Kit: Put together a spa kit with homemade bath bombs, scented candles, a relaxing playlist, and a soft bathrobe. Include instructions for creating a spa-like atmosphere at home.

2. Cocktail Kit: Create a cocktail kit with a selection of mini liquor bottles, mixers, and cocktail recipes. Add some fun garnishes like citrus slices or cocktail umbrellas.

3. Gardening Kit: Assemble a gardening kit with seeds, gardening gloves, small pots, and soil. Include a guide with tips for growing different plants.

By exploring these creative and affordable homemade gift ideas, you can make your holiday presents extra special without breaking the bank. Remember, the most important thing is the thought and love you put into each gift. Happy crafting and happy holidays!

Conclusion

In conclusion, this chapter has provided valuable insights into the world of DIY gifts and decorations for the holiday season. By exploring creative and affordable homemade gift ideas, you have the opportunity to not only save money but also add a personal touch to your gifts. Designing budget-friendly holiday decorations allows you to create a festive atmosphere without breaking the bank. Additionally, involving family and friends in DIY projects can make the process more enjoyable and create lasting memories.

As you embark on your DIY journey, remember that the true value of these homemade gifts and decorations lies in the love and effort you put into them. Whether you're making a heartfelt gift or crafting a beautiful ornament, the recipient will appreciate the thoughtfulness behind it. So, embrace your creativity, have fun, and enjoy the process of creating unique and meaningful gifts and decorations for the holiday season. Happy crafting!

CHAPTER 5 :
MAXIMIZING YOUR
SAVINGS

Welcome to Chapter 5 of 'Spend Less and Get More: Your Ultimate Holiday Guide.' In this chapter, we delve into the art of maximizing your savings, equipping you with strategies and techniques to make every dollar count during the holiday season. Whether you're a seasoned bargain hunter or new to the world of frugal living, this chapter will provide you with valuable insights and tips to help you stretch your holiday budget further than ever before.

Unlocking the Power of Cashback and Rewards Programs

In today's world, where every penny counts, maximizing your savings during the holiday season is crucial. One of the most effective ways to do this is by taking advantage of cashback and rewards programs. These programs offer you the opportunity to earn money back or accumulate points that can be redeemed for discounts, gift cards, or other incentives. Let's dive into how you can unlock the power of these programs and make the most out of your holiday shopping.

Subsection 1: Understanding Cashback Programs

Cashback programs are designed to reward you for your purchases. They work by partnering with retailers and offering a percentage of your total purchase price back to you. The percentage varies depending on the program and the retailer, but it can range from 1% to as high as 10% or more. To take advantage of cashback programs, follow these steps:

1. Research and Sign Up: Start by researching different cashback programs available in your country or region. Look for popular ones like Rakuten, Honey, or Swagbucks. Once you've identified a few programs, sign up for them using your email address or social media accounts.

2. Install Browser Extensions: Many cashback programs offer browser extensions that can automatically notify you when you're on a website that partners with the program. These extensions make it easy to activate cashback offers without having to go through the program's website every time.

3. Shop Through the Cashback Portal: When you're ready to make a purchase online, access the retailer's website through the cashback program's portal. This step is crucial because it ensures that your purchase is tracked and eligible for cashback. If you skip this step, you might miss out on valuable savings.

4. Accumulate and Redeem: As you make purchases through cashback programs, your savings will accumulate. Once you reach a certain threshold, you can redeem your earnings in the form of cash, gift cards, or other rewards. Check the program's terms and conditions to understand how and when you can redeem your earnings.

Subsection 2: Unleashing the Power of Rewards Programs

Rewards programs are similar to cashback programs but often offer additional perks and benefits. These programs encourage loyalty by providing exclusive discounts, early access to sales, and personalized offers. To make the most out of rewards programs, follow these steps:

1. Identify Relevant Programs: Start by identifying rewards programs that align with your shopping habits and preferences. Look for programs offered by your favorite retailers, airlines, hotels, and credit cards. Consider joining multiple programs to maximize your benefits.

2. Understand the Program's Structure: Each rewards program has its own structure and rules. Take the time to understand how points are earned, how they can be redeemed, and any limitations or restrictions that apply. Some programs offer points based on your spending, while others provide bonuses for specific actions like referring friends or completing surveys.

3. Use Your Rewards Strategically: Once you've accumulated a significant number of rewards points, it's time to put them to good use. Look for opportunities to redeem your points for discounts, freebies, or upgrades. For example, if you've earned enough points with an airline rewards program, you might be able to book a free flight or upgrade to business class.

4. Keep an Eye on Special Offers: Rewards programs often run special promotions and limited-time offers. Stay informed about these opportunities by subscribing to program newsletters, following them on social media, or enabling notifications on their mobile apps. By taking advantage of these offers, you can maximize your savings even further.

By utilizing cashback and rewards programs effectively, you can significantly reduce your holiday expenses and get more value for your money. Take the time to research and sign up for these programs today, and watch your savings grow with every purchase you make. Remember, every little bit adds up, so start unlocking the power of cashback and rewards programs this holiday season!

Mastering the Art of Price Protection and Price Matching

In today's world, where prices seem to be constantly fluctuating, it can be challenging to keep up with the best deals and discounts. However, with a little knowledge and strategic planning, you can become a master of price protection and price matching, allowing you to maximize your savings during the holiday season.

1. Understanding Price Protection Policies

Price protection policies are a valuable tool that many retailers offer to ensure that you get the best possible deal on your purchases. These policies typically allow you to claim a refund if the price of an item drops within a specified time frame after your purchase. By taking advantage of price protection policies, you can confidently make your holiday purchases knowing that you won't miss out on any future discounts.

2. Researching Retailers with Price Matching

Price matching is another fantastic way to save money during the holiday season. Many retailers offer price matching, which means that if you find a lower price for an identical item at a competitor's store, they will match that price. This can be a game-changer when it comes to maximizing your savings. Spend some time researching retailers that offer price matching and familiarize yourself with their policies.

3. Keeping Track of Price Drops

To make the most of price protection policies and price matching, you need to stay vigilant and keep track of price drops. This can be a time-consuming process, but it can result in significant savings. Consider using price tracking tools and apps that can help you monitor price fluctuations and notify you when an item you're interested in goes on sale or drops in price. These tools can save you both time and money by doing the work for you.

4. Strategically Timing Your Purchases

Timing is everything when it comes to maximizing your savings. Keep an eye out for sales events, such as Black Friday, Cyber Monday, and pre-holiday sales. These are prime opportunities to score incredible deals. Additionally, consider purchasing items during off-peak seasons or times when demand is lower. Retailers are more likely to offer discounts and promotions during these periods to attract customers.

5. Utilizing Coupons and Promo Codes

Coupons and promo codes can be your secret weapons for saving money during the holiday season. Look for coupons in newspapers, magazines, and online coupon websites. Sign up for retailers' newsletters to receive exclusive discounts and promo codes. Additionally, consider using browser extensions that automatically apply coupon codes at checkout, saving you both time and money.

6. Bundling and Stacking Discounts

Once you've mastered the art of utilizing coupons and promo codes, take it a step further by bundling and stacking discounts. Look for opportunities to combine multiple discounts to maximize your savings. For example, if a retailer allows you to use a store coupon along with a manufacturer's coupon, take advantage of both. Additionally, consider bundling purchases to reach minimum spending thresholds for free shipping or additional discounts.

By understanding and implementing these strategies, you can become a savvy shopper who knows how to make the most of price protection policies, price matching, timing, and discounts. Take the time to research, plan ahead, and stay organized, and you'll be amazed at how much you can save during the holiday season.

Maximizing Your Savings: Strategies for Smart Shopping

When it comes to holiday shopping, finding ways to maximize your savings is key. By employing a few clever strategies, you can stretch your budget further and get the most out of every dollar you spend. In this section, we will explore various techniques that will help you become a savvy shopper and save money during the holiday season.

Subsection 1: Taking Advantage of Cashback and Rewards Programs

One of the easiest ways to save money while shopping is by utilizing cashback and rewards programs. Many retailers offer these programs, which allow you to earn a percentage of your purchase as cashback or rewards points. These programs can be a great way to earn back some of the money you spend and get additional benefits.

To make the most of cashback and rewards programs, consider the following tips:

1. Research and compare different programs: Not all cashback and rewards programs are created equal. Take the time to research and compare the programs offered by different retailers to find the ones that offer the best rewards and benefits.

2. Sign up for multiple programs: Don't limit yourself to just one cashback or rewards program. Sign up for multiple programs to maximize your earning potential. Just make sure to keep track of your memberships and understand the terms and conditions of each program.

3. Stack your rewards: Some retailers allow you to stack rewards from different programs. This means that you can earn cashback or rewards points from multiple programs on a single purchase. Take advantage of this by using multiple programs to earn even more savings.

Subsection 2: Utilizing Price Protection Policies and Price Matching

Another effective way to save money during the holiday season is by utilizing price protection policies and price matching. Many retailers offer these policies to ensure that you get the best price possible on your purchases. Here's how you can make the most of these policies:

1. Understand the price protection policies: Familiarize yourself with the price protection policies of the retailers you frequent. These policies usually allow you to request a refund if the price of an item drops within a certain time frame after your purchase.

2. Keep an eye on prices: Monitor the prices of the items you plan to buy. If you notice that the price has dropped within the specified time frame, reach out to the retailer and request a refund.

3. Take advantage of price matching: Price matching is when a retailer matches the price of a product offered by a competitor. Before making a purchase, check if the retailer you're buying from offers price matching. If they do, compare prices from different retailers and take advantage of this policy to get the best deal.

Subsection 3: Planning Ahead for Post-Holiday Sales and Clearance

While the holiday season is known for its sales and promotions, the real deals often come after the holidays. Planning ahead for post-holiday sales and clearance events can help you save a significant amount of money. Here's how you can do it:

1. Make a list of items you need: Before the holiday season begins, make a list of items you need or want to buy. This can include anything from clothing and electronics to home decor and kitchen appliances. By having a clear list, you can focus on finding the best deals for those specific items.

2. Research sales and clearance events: Keep an eye out for sales and clearance events that happen after the holidays. Many retailers offer deep discounts to clear out their inventory and make room for new merchandise. Research the dates and details of these events and mark them on your calendar.

3. Prioritize your purchases: Not all post-holiday sales are created equal. Some may offer better discounts on certain items than others. Prioritize your purchases based on the deals available. If you find a great deal on an item you need, consider buying it even if it's not on your immediate list.

By implementing these strategies, you can make the most of your holiday shopping and maximize your savings. Remember, being a smart shopper is all about planning ahead, researching your options, and taking advantage of the various programs and policies offered by retailers. Happy shopping and happy saving!

Maximizing Your Savings: Key Takeaways and Actionable Advice

In this chapter, we explored various strategies to help you maximize your savings during the holiday season. By taking advantage of cashback and rewards programs, you can earn money back on your purchases and save even more. Additionally, utilizing price protection policies and price matching ensures that you get the best deal available, even after making a purchase. Lastly, planning ahead for post-holiday sales and clearance allows you to snag incredible deals on items you may have missed during the holiday rush.

As you move forward, remember these key takeaways:

1. Research and sign up for cashback and rewards programs to earn money back on your holiday purchases.
2. Familiarize yourself with the price protection policies of your favorite stores and take advantage of price matching to guarantee the lowest price.
3. Keep an eye on post-holiday sales and clearance events for fantastic deals on items you may have wanted but couldn't afford during the holiday season.

By implementing these strategies, you can make the most of your holiday budget and truly maximize your savings. Happy shopping!

CHAPTER 6 :
ALTERNATIVE
GIFT-GIVING

Welcome to Chapter 6 of 'Spend Less and Get More: Your Ultimate Holiday Guide.' In this chapter, we will delve into the transformative world of alternative gift-giving, where we shift our focus from material possessions to the power of creating lasting memories and meaningful experiences. As the holiday season approaches, we often find ourselves caught up in the frenzy of shopping malls and online deals, searching for that perfect gift to impress our loved ones. We get lost in a sea of consumerism, forgetting the true essence of the holidays - the joy of giving and the warmth of connection. It's time to break free from the chains of materialism and embrace a new approach that will not only save us money but also bring us closer to our loved ones.

Unwrapping the Joy of Non-Material Gifts

In a world that often equates happiness and joy with material possessions, it's time to challenge the status quo and discover the magic of non-material gifts. These gifts have the power to create lasting memories, deepen relationships, and leave a positive impact on both the giver and the receiver. In this chapter, we will explore various non-material gift options that will bring joy and meaning to your holiday season.

Subsection 1: Experiences That Create Lifelong Memories

When it comes to gift-giving, experiences can be the most valuable and cherished presents. Instead of wrapping up a physical item, consider giving the gift of a shared experience. Whether it's a cooking class, concert tickets, a spa day, or an adventurous outdoor activity, experiences have the power to create lifelong memories. These gifts go beyond the material and allow you to spend quality time together, strengthening the bonds of friendship and family.

Subsection 2: Quality Time Over Material Possessions

In a world inundated with material possessions, it's easy to lose sight of what truly matters. This holiday season, let's shift our focus from accumulating things to spending quality time with our loved ones. Instead of buying expensive gadgets or the latest trend, consider giving the gift of your time. Plan a movie night, game night, or a simple picnic in the park. These moments of connection and laughter are priceless and will be remembered long after the holiday season is over.

Subsection 3: Supporting Local Businesses and Artisans

One of the most meaningful ways to give non-material gifts is by supporting local businesses and artisans. This not only adds a personal touch to your gifts but also helps to stimulate the local economy. Seek out unique and handcrafted items that reflect the talents and creativity of local artisans. Whether it's a piece of handmade jewelry, a hand-painted artwork, or a jar of locally sourced honey, these gifts not only bring joy to the receiver but also support the artistic community and preserve traditional craftsmanship.

Subsection 4: Volunteering and Giving Back

The holiday season is a time of giving, and what better way to celebrate than by giving back to your community? Volunteering your time or making a donation in someone's name can be a powerful way to show your love and appreciation. Consider volunteering at a local shelter, organizing a neighborhood food drive, or making a charitable donation to a cause that aligns with the values of your loved ones. These acts of kindness not only make a difference in the lives of others but also bring a sense of fulfillment and joy to the giver.

Subsection 5: The Gift of Knowledge and Learning

Education is a gift that keeps on giving. Instead of opting for material possessions, consider giving the gift of knowledge and learning. This could include enrolling your loved ones in a cooking class, a photography workshop, or a language course. By investing in their personal growth and development, you are giving them the tools to explore new passions, expand their horizons, and create a more fulfilling life.

Subsection 6: Acts of Service and Kindness

Sometimes the most valuable gifts we can give are acts of service and kindness. Offer to babysit for a busy friend, help an elderly neighbor with their grocery shopping, or prepare a homemade meal for a family in need. These acts of service not only show your love and care but also inspire others to pay it forward. By spreading kindness, we create a ripple effect of positivity and make the world a better place.

Subsection 7: Thoughtful Letters and Expressions of Love

In a digital age where communication is often reduced to a quick text or email, the art of letter-writing has become increasingly rare. Take the time to write a heartfelt letter to your loved ones, expressing your love, gratitude, and appreciation. Share your favorite memories, funny anecdotes, and words of encouragement. These letters become cherished keepsakes that can be read and reread, bringing joy and comfort for years to come.

Subsection 8: Sharing Your Talents and Skills

We all have unique talents and skills that can be shared with others. Consider offering your expertise as a gift. Whether you're a skilled photographer offering a family photoshoot, a musician giving a private concert, or a baker sharing your delicious homemade treats, these gifts showcase your talents and create meaningful experiences for others. By sharing your gifts, you not only bring joy to the receiver but also inspire them to explore their own passions and talents.

Subsection 9: Acts of Environmental Consciousness

As we become more aware of the impact of our actions on the environment, non-material gifts that promote sustainability and environmental consciousness are gaining popularity. Consider giving gifts such as potted plants, reusable water bottles, or eco-friendly household items. These gifts not only reduce waste but also inspire others to adopt more sustainable practices in their daily lives.

Subsection 10: The Power of Presence

Perhaps the most precious gift of all is the gift of your presence. In a world filled with distractions and busyness, simply being fully present with your loved ones is a gift in itself. Put away your phone, engage in meaningful conversations, and create space for deep connections. Your undivided attention and genuine presence are invaluable and will be appreciated far beyond any material gift.

By embracing the joy of non-material gifts, we can create a holiday season filled with meaning, connection, and happiness. Let's shift our focus from material possessions to experiences, quality time, and acts of kindness. Together, we can make this holiday season truly magical for ourselves and our loved ones. Remember, the greatest gift you can give is the gift of your heart.

Conclusion: Embracing the Joy of Alternative Gift-Giving

In this chapter, we have delved into the world of alternative gift-giving, exploring the many ways in which we can move beyond material possessions and embrace experiences, quality time, and support for local businesses and artisans. By shifting our focus from the material to the meaningful, we not only reduce our spending but also enhance the joy and satisfaction we derive from the holiday season.

Throughout this chapter, we have discussed various non-material gift options, such as creating memories through shared experiences, offering our time and skills, and supporting local businesses and artisans. These alternatives provide a unique opportunity to express our love and appreciation for others in a more thoughtful and personal manner.

By emphasizing experiences and quality time over material possessions, we can forge stronger connections with our loved ones, creating lasting memories that will far outlast any physical gift. Whether it's a family outing, a day spent volunteering together, or a heartfelt conversation, these moments of connection truly embody the spirit of the holiday season.

Furthermore, by supporting local businesses and artisans, we not only contribute to the local economy but also help sustain the unique crafts and traditions of our communities. It is through these thoughtful choices that we can make a positive impact and foster a sense of community and togetherness during the holiday season.

As we wrap up this chapter, I encourage you to embrace the joy and fulfillment that comes from alternative gift-giving. Consider the experiences you can share, the quality time you can spend, and the local businesses and artisans you can support. By doing so, you will not only spend less but also create a more meaningful and memorable holiday season for yourself and those around you.

Remember, the true value of a gift lies not in its price tag, but in the thought, love, and care that went into choosing it. So, let us embark on this journey of alternative gift-giving, and may it bring us closer to the essence of the holiday spirit.

CHAPTER 7 : MANAGING HOLIDAY TRAVEL EXPENSES

Welcome to Chapter 7 of 'Spend Less and Get More: Holiday Guide.' In this chapter, we will explore valuable strategies and insider tips to help you manage your holiday travel expenses without compromising on the joy and excitement of your vacation. Whether you're planning a trip to visit loved ones or embarking on a well-deserved getaway, we understand the importance of keeping your travel costs in check.

Travel expenses can often be a significant part of your holiday budget, but fear not, as we have got you covered. We will guide you through the process of finding affordable flights and accommodations, saving on transportation costs, and making the most of travel rewards and loyalty programs. By implementing these strategies, you'll be able to enjoy your holiday to the fullest while keeping your wallet happy.

Mastering the Art of Affordable Travel

Traveling during the holiday season can be an expensive endeavor, but with the right strategies in place, you can manage your holiday travel expenses and still enjoy a memorable vacation. In this section, we will explore various tips and tricks to help you find affordable flights and accommodations, save on transportation costs, and make the most of travel rewards and loyalty programs.

Subsection 1: Finding Affordable Flights

When it comes to booking flights for your holiday travel, timing is everything. Start by planning your trip well in advance, as last-minute bookings tend to be more expensive. Additionally, consider the following strategies:

1. Flexibility is Key: Being flexible with your travel dates can save you a significant amount of money. Check different departure and arrival dates to find the most affordable options. Sometimes, flying on the actual holiday can result in lower fares.

2. Compare Prices: Utilize online travel aggregators and search engines to compare prices from different airlines. Keep an eye out for flash sales and special promotions. Don't forget to check the airline's official website, as they may offer exclusive deals.

3. Opt for Connecting Flights: Direct flights are convenient, but they can also be more expensive. Consider booking connecting flights to save money. However, be mindful of layover durations and ensure you have enough time to make your connections.

4. Consider Alternate Airports: Flying into or out of smaller regional airports can sometimes be cheaper than major international airports. Explore all available options to find the best deals.

Subsection 2: Affordable Accommodations

Finding affordable accommodations during the holiday season can be challenging, but with these strategies, you can secure a comfortable place to stay without breaking the bank:

1. Book Early: Just like with flights, booking your accommodations well in advance can often result in lower prices. Popular hotels and vacation rentals tend to fill up quickly during the holiday season, so make your reservations as early as possible.

2. Consider Alternative Accommodations: Instead of staying at traditional hotels, explore other options like vacation rentals, hostels, or even house-swapping. These alternatives can offer unique experiences and often come at a lower cost.

3. Location Matters: Consider staying slightly outside the main tourist areas to find more affordable accommodations. Utilize public transportation or ride-sharing services to easily access the popular attractions.

4. Look for Package Deals: Some travel websites offer package deals that include both flights and accommodations. These packages can often save you money compared to booking them separately.

Subsection 3: Saving on Transportation Costs

Transportation costs can add up quickly during your holiday travels. Here are some tips to help you save on transportation expenses:

1. Public Transportation: Utilize public transportation systems whenever possible. They are often more cost-effective than taxis or rental cars. Research the public transportation options available at your destination before you arrive.

2. Carpooling: If you're traveling with a group or visiting family and friends, consider carpooling to reduce transportation costs. Sharing the expenses with others can significantly lower your overall spending.

3. Walk or Bike: If your destination is within walking or biking distance, leave the car behind and enjoy some exercise while exploring the area. Not only will you save money, but you'll also have a chance to immerse yourself in the local culture.

4. Use Ride-Sharing Apps: If public transportation is not readily available or convenient, consider using ride-sharing apps like Uber or Lyft. These services often offer lower fares compared to traditional taxis.

Subsection 4: Making the Most of Travel
Rewards and Loyalty Programs

If you frequently travel during the holidays, it's worth
exploring travel rewards and loyalty programs to maximize
your savings. Consider the following strategies:

1. Sign up for Frequent Flyer Programs: Join airlines'
frequent flyer programs to earn miles every time you fly.
Accumulated miles can be redeemed for free flights or
upgrades, helping you save money on future travels.

2. Credit Card Rewards: Opt for credit cards that offer travel
rewards. These cards often provide benefits like airline miles,
hotel discounts, or cashback on travel-related expenses.

3. Hotel Loyalty Programs: Sign up for hotel loyalty programs
to enjoy exclusive perks, such as discounted rates, room
upgrades, or late check-outs. Take advantage of these
programs to save on your holiday accommodations.

4. Travel Credit Cards: Consider getting a travel credit card
that offers points or miles for every dollar spent on travel-
related purchases. These cards often come with additional
benefits like travel insurance or access to airport lounges.

By implementing these strategies, you can effectively
manage your holiday travel expenses and make the most
of your vacation budget. Remember, the key is to plan
ahead, be flexible, and explore all available options. With
a little effort and smart decision-making, you can enjoy
a memorable holiday without breaking the bank.

Key Takeaways and Actionable Advice

In this chapter, we explored various strategies for
managing holiday travel expenses. Here are the key

takeaways and actionable advice to help you spend less and get more during your holiday trips:

1. Finding Affordable Flights and Accommodations:
- Use flight comparison websites to compare prices and find the best deals.
- Consider booking accommodations through platforms that offer discounted rates or stay in budget-friendly accommodations like hostels or home-sharing services.

2. Saving on Transportation Costs:
- Opt for public transportation or carpooling options to save on transportation expenses.
- Research and compare the prices of different transportation options like trains, buses, and rental cars.

3. Making the Most of Travel Rewards and Loyalty Programs:
- Join loyalty programs offered by airlines, hotels, and car rental companies to earn points and enjoy exclusive benefits.
- Utilize travel reward credit cards to earn points on your everyday purchases and redeem them for free flights, hotel stays, or upgrades.

By implementing these strategies and taking advantage of travel rewards and loyalty programs, you can significantly reduce your holiday travel expenses while still enjoying memorable experiences. Remember, planning ahead, being flexible with your travel dates, and being mindful of your budget are key to making the most of your holiday trips. Happy travels!

CHAPTER 8 : HOSTING ON A BUDGET

*Hosting on a Budget: Creating
Memorable Gatherings Without
Breaking the Bank*

Welcome to Chapter 8 of 'Spend Less and Get More: Your Ultimate Holiday Guide.' In this chapter, we will dive into the art of hosting on a budget, where we aim to show you how to create memorable gatherings without breaking the bank. We understand that hosting a holiday event can be both exciting and daunting, especially when it comes to managing the expenses. But fear not, because we are here to share with you our expert tips and tricks that will help you become a master of budget-friendly hosting.

In today's world, where the pressure to impress can often overshadow the true meaning of the holiday season, it's essential to remember that the joy of hosting lies in the warmth and connection shared with loved ones, not the extravagance of the event. By embracing the spirit of simplicity and creativity, you can create an unforgettable experience for your guests while staying within your budget.

One of the first steps in planning a budget-friendly holiday gathering is to set a realistic budget. By determining how much you are willing to spend, you can make informed decisions about the various elements of your gathering, from the menu to the decorations. We will guide you through this process and provide you with practical strategies to make the most of your budget.

Potluck parties have become increasingly popular in recent years, and for good reason. Not only do they allow guests to contribute to the meal, easing the burden on the host, but they also create a sense of community and shared responsibility. We will explore different potluck party ideas, including themed potlucks and recipe exchanges, that will add an element of excitement and variety to your gathering.

Additionally, we will delve into the world of do-it-yourself (DIY) party ideas. From handmade decorations to personalized party favors, DIY projects can add a unique touch to your event without breaking the bank. We will provide you with step-by-step instructions and creative ideas that will inspire you to unleash your inner artist and create a truly memorable experience for your guests.

But hosting on a budget is not just about the food and decorations. It's also about creating an atmosphere that fosters connection and joy. We will share tips on how to entertain your guests without spending a fortune, from organizing budget-friendly games and activities to curating a playlist that sets the mood.

So, whether you are hosting a small gathering or a larger party, this chapter will equip you with the knowledge and inspiration to create a memorable event without draining your bank account. Get ready to embark on a journey of creativity and resourcefulness as we explore the wonderful world of hosting on a budget. Let's make your next holiday gathering a truly magical and affordable experience!

Hosting on a Budget: Creating Memorable Gatherings without Breaking the Bank

Planning a budget-friendly holiday gathering can be a fun and rewarding experience. With a little creativity and smart decision-making, you can create memorable moments without putting a strain on your wallet. In this section, we'll explore various tips and ideas to help you host a fantastic holiday gathering on a budget.

Subsection 1: Set a Realistic Budget

Before you start planning your holiday gathering, it's essential to set a realistic budget. Determine how much you can comfortably spend on food, decorations, and other essentials. By having a clear budget in mind, you'll be able to make informed decisions and avoid overspending.

Subsection 2: Host a Potluck Party

One fantastic way to save money and make your holiday gathering more interactive is by hosting a potluck party. Instead of shouldering the entire burden of cooking, invite your guests to bring a dish or beverage to share. Not only will this help you save on food expenses, but it will also add a diverse range of flavors to your gathering.

Subsection 3: DIY Decorations

Decorating your home for the holidays doesn't have to be expensive. Embrace your creativity and make DIY decorations using materials you already have or can easily acquire at a low cost. Consider making paper snowflakes, creating a centerpiece using pine cones and branches, or repurposing old ornaments. DIY decorations not only save you money but also add a personal touch to your gathering.

Subsection 4: Entertainment on a Budget

Entertaining your guests without breaking the bank can be achieved through various budget-friendly activities. Plan interactive games like charades or a holiday-themed trivia quiz. You can also organize a movie night with classic holiday films or ask your musically inclined friends to bring their instruments for an impromptu jam session. The key is to focus on activities that are enjoyable and memorable, rather than expensive.

Subsection 5: Creative Gift Exchanges

Instead of traditional gift exchanges, consider introducing creative and budget-friendly alternatives. For example, you can organize a white elephant gift exchange, where each participant brings a quirky or humorous gift. Another idea is to have a homemade gift exchange, where everyone creates something unique and heartfelt. These alternatives not only add excitement to your gathering but also reduce the financial burden on everyone involved.

Subsection 6: Thrifty Table Settings

Creating an elegant table setting doesn't have to cost a fortune. Look for affordable table linens, such as tablecloths and napkins, at discount stores or thrift shops. Consider using mismatched vintage china or opting for reusable and eco-friendly options like bamboo plates and utensils. With a little creativity and resourcefulness, you can create a beautiful table setting without breaking the bank.

Subsection 7: Stretch Your Beverages

Beverages can be a significant expense when hosting a gathering. To save money, consider serving homemade punch, infused water, or signature cocktails instead of purchasing expensive pre-made drinks. You can also encourage your guests to bring their favorite beverages to share. By stretching your beverages, you'll be able to provide refreshments without depleting your budget.

Subsection 8: Plan Ahead for Sales and Coupons

To maximize your savings, plan your holiday gathering well in advance and keep an eye out for sales and coupons. Take advantage of seasonal discounts on food, decorations, and

OLIVIA FRUGAL

other party essentials. Sign up for newsletters or loyalty programs at your favorite stores to receive exclusive discounts and promotions. With careful planning, you can snag great deals and save money on your holiday gathering.

Subsection 9: Collaborate with Friends and Family

Consider teaming up with friends or family members who are also planning holiday gatherings. By pooling resources and sharing expenses, you can create a larger and more festive gathering without increasing the financial burden on any one person. Collaborating with loved ones not only saves money but also strengthens the sense of community and togetherness during the holiday season.

Subsection 10: Express Gratitude

Finally, remember that the true spirit of the holidays is not about extravagant spending or lavish parties. It's about expressing gratitude and cherishing the company of loved ones. Regardless of the size or scale of your holiday gathering, focus on creating a warm and welcoming atmosphere where everyone feels appreciated and valued. By prioritizing the connections and memories made, you'll find that hosting on a budget can still result in a joyful and fulfilling experience.

In conclusion, hosting a budget-friendly holiday gathering is entirely possible with a little planning, creativity, and resourcefulness. Set a realistic budget, consider hosting a potluck party, make DIY decorations, plan budget-friendly entertainment, explore creative gift exchanges, create thrifty table settings, stretch your beverages, plan ahead for sales and coupons, collaborate with friends and family, and prioritize gratitude. By implementing these strategies, you can create unforgettable holiday gatherings without breaking the bank.

Hosting on a Budget: Creating

Memorable Gatherings Without Breaking the Bank

Planning a budget-friendly holiday gathering is not only possible but can also be a fun and rewarding experience. With a little creativity and strategic thinking, you can create memorable moments for your guests without straining your wallet. In this section, we will explore various ideas and tips to help you host a fabulous holiday gathering on a budget.

Subsection 1: Planning a Budget-Friendly Holiday Gathering

1.1 Set a Realistic Budget
When it comes to hosting a holiday gathering on a budget, the first step is to determine how much you are willing to spend. Take into account your overall financial situation and allocate a specific amount for the event. This will serve as your guiding principle throughout the planning process.

1.2 Keep the Guest List Intimate
One effective way to save money on your holiday gathering is to keep the guest list intimate. By inviting only close friends and family, you can create a warm and cozy atmosphere while minimizing expenses. Remember, the focus should be on quality time spent with loved ones rather than the number of guests.

1.3 Embrace a Potluck Party
A potluck party is an excellent option for hosting a budget-friendly holiday gathering. Instead of shouldering the entire burden of preparing a feast, invite your guests to contribute a dish or two. This not only reduces your workload but also adds variety to the menu. Encourage guests to bring their favorite holiday recipes and share the joy of cooking together.

1.4 DIY Party Decorations
Decorating your venue can be a significant expense, but it doesn't have to be. Get creative and make your own party decorations using inexpensive materials such as

paper, ribbons, and ornaments. Consider making festive centerpieces, garlands, and table settings using items you already have at home. This personal touch adds charm and uniqueness to your gathering while keeping costs low.

Subsection 2: Potluck and DIY Party Ideas

2.1 Theme-based Potluck
Adding a theme to your potluck gathering can make it even more exciting. Choose a theme that reflects the holiday season, such as 'Winter Wonderland' or 'Ugly Sweater Party.' Ask your guests to align their dishes and outfits with the theme, creating a fun and festive atmosphere without spending a fortune.

2.2 Dessert Extravaganza
If your friends and family have a sweet tooth, consider organizing a dessert potluck. Ask each guest to bring their favorite dessert, and let the sugar-filled celebration begin. From cookies and cakes to pies and pastries, there will be something for everyone to enjoy.

2.3 DIY Cocktail Party
Hosting a cocktail party can be expensive, but with a DIY approach, it can be budget-friendly and impressive. Create a signature holiday cocktail and ask guests to bring their favorite spirits or mixers. Provide a selection of garnishes and create a festive drink station where guests can personalize their beverages. This interactive experience adds a touch of elegance to your gathering without breaking the bank.

Subsection 3: Decorating and Entertaining Without Breaking the Bank

3.1 Utilize Natural Elements
Nature offers an abundance of free and beautiful decorations. Incorporate pinecones, holly branches, and evergreen sprigs into your holiday decor. Arrange them in vases, create wreaths, or use them as table centerpieces. These natural elements add a rustic and cozy touch to your gathering without costing a penny.

3.2 Candlelit Ambiance

Candles create a warm and inviting atmosphere, perfect for a holiday gathering. Use a combination of pillar candles, tea lights, and candle lanterns to create a cozy ambiance. Place them strategically around your venue, on tables, and near the entrance to welcome your guests. Opt for unscented candles to avoid overwhelming food aromas.

3.3 Music and Entertainment

Entertainment doesn't have to be expensive to be enjoyable. Create a holiday playlist with your favorite festive tunes and play it throughout the gathering. Encourage your musically-inclined guests to bring their instruments and have an impromptu jam session. You can also organize fun and interactive games that require minimal or no materials, such as charades or holiday-themed trivia.

Subsection 4: Conclusion

Hosting a holiday gathering on a budget is all about finding the perfect balance between creativity, resourcefulness, and joy. By planning ahead, embracing a potluck approach, and getting creative with decorations and entertainment, you can create a memorable experience for your guests without breaking the bank. Remember, it's the thought and effort you put into the gathering that truly matters, not the amount of money spent.

In the next chapter, we will explore strategies to avoid post-holiday debt and ensure a financially stress-free start to the new year.

Spend Less and Get More: Hosting on a Budget

In conclusion, hosting a budget-friendly holiday gathering doesn't mean sacrificing the joy and warmth of the season. By following the tips and ideas discussed in this chapter, you can create a memorable event without breaking the bank.

First and foremost, proper planning is key. Set a budget and stick to it, considering all the necessary expenses such as food, decorations, and entertainment.

Embrace the concept of a potluck or DIY party, where guests can contribute their favorite dishes or participate in fun activities together. This not only eases the financial burden but also adds an element of shared involvement and creativity to the gathering.

Next, explore the world of DIY decorations and entertainment. With a little creativity, you can transform everyday items into festive decor and create a joyful ambiance without spending a fortune. Consider using natural elements like pinecones, branches, and candles to add warmth and charm to your space.

Remember, the focus of any holiday gathering should be on the people and the experiences shared. Create meaningful moments with your loved ones through thoughtful conversations, games, or even a simple movie night. It's not about how much money you spend but rather the quality of time you spend together.

Lastly, don't forget to leverage the power of technology and social media. Use online resources to find budget-friendly recipes, decoration ideas, and even free entertainment options. Share your experiences and connect with others who have similar interests and goals. By doing so, you not only expand your knowledge but also create a supportive community around your budget-friendly approach to hosting.

In summary, hosting on a budget is all about being resourceful, creative, and mindful of your spending. With careful planning, embracing the concept of shared contributions, and leveraging the power of DIY and technology, you can create a holiday gathering that is not only affordable but also meaningful and enjoyable for all. So go ahead, start planning, and make this holiday season a memorable one without breaking the bank!

CHAPTER 9 : AVOIDING POST-HOLIDAY DEBT

Avoiding Post-Holiday Debt: A
Path to Financial Freedom

Welcome to Chapter 9 of 'Spend Less and Get More: Your Ultimate Holiday Guide.' In this chapter, we delve into the crucial topic of avoiding post-holiday debt and provide you with practical strategies to ensure a financially secure start to the new year. We understand that the joy of the holiday season can sometimes be overshadowed by the burden of excessive debt. That's why we are here to help you navigate through this potential pitfall and guide you towards a path of financial freedom.

The holiday season is undeniably a time of celebration, filled with warmth, love, and cherished moments with family and friends. However, it is also a period notorious for overspending, impulsive purchases, and the accumulation of credit card debt. According to recent surveys, many individuals find themselves carrying the weight of holiday debt well into the following year, hindering their ability to achieve financial goals and causing unnecessary stress.

But fear not! Our expert advice and practical tips will empower you to take control of your post-holiday finances and avoid falling into the debt trap. We will show you how to create a plan for paying off your holiday debt effectively, so you can start the new year with a clean slate.

One of the first steps in avoiding post-holiday debt is to assess the extent of your financial situation. We will guide you through the process of evaluating your holiday spending and help you gain a clear understanding of your current debt. By facing these numbers head-on, you can develop a realistic plan to tackle your debt and regain financial stability.

In addition to creating a repayment plan, we will discuss strategies for avoiding overspending during post-holiday sales. It can be tempting to continue shopping when faced with enticing discounts and promotions, but we will teach you how to resist the urge and stay focused on your financial goals. We believe that a mindful approach to spending during this time is key to preventing further debt and ensuring long-term financial well-being.

To assist you on your journey towards financial freedom, we will introduce you to various budgeting tools and resources that can help you stay on track. From mobile apps to online calculators, these tools will enable you to monitor your expenses, set realistic financial targets, and make informed decisions about your spending habits. Armed with these resources, you will have the knowledge and support necessary to overcome any financial challenges that may arise.

By following the advice provided in this chapter, you will not only avoid post-holiday debt but also develop healthy financial habits that will benefit you throughout the year. We firmly believe that with the right mindset and effective strategies, you can achieve financial freedom and enjoy a stress-free start to the new year.

So, without further ado, let's dive into Chapter 9 and embark on a journey towards a debt-free and financially secure future!

Creating a Plan for Paying

Off Holiday Debt

The holiday season is a time of joy and celebration, but it can also be a period of financial stress for many people. Overspending during the holidays can lead to post-holiday debt that can linger long after the decorations have been put away. To avoid the pitfalls of post-holiday debt, it is essential to create a plan for paying off your holiday expenses. In this section, we will explore effective strategies to help you tackle your debt and regain control of your finances.

Subsection 1: Assessing Your Holiday Debt

Before you can create a plan to pay off your holiday debt, it is crucial to assess the extent of your financial obligations. Take a moment to gather all your credit card statements, receipts, and any other relevant documents that detail your holiday spending. Calculate the total amount you owe and make a list of all the debts you need to address.

Subsection 2: Prioritizing Your Debts

Once you have a clear picture of your holiday debt, it's time to prioritize which debts to tackle first. Start by identifying the debts with the highest interest rates, as these are the ones that can cost you the most in the long run. By focusing on high-interest debts first, you can save money on interest charges and pay off your debts more quickly. Additionally, consider any debts that are past due or have penalties attached to them and prioritize resolving those as well.

Subsection 3: Creating a Repayment Plan

Now that you know which debts to prioritize, it's time to create a repayment plan. Start by determining how much you can afford to allocate toward debt repayment each month. Look at your current monthly income and expenses and identify areas where you can cut back to free up additional funds. It may require making temporary sacrifices, such as reducing dining out or entertainment expenses, but remember that it's a short-term measure to regain control of your finances.

Next, allocate your available funds to your prioritized debts. Consider using the debt avalanche or debt snowball method to guide your repayment strategy. With the debt avalanche method, you focus on paying off the debt with the highest interest rate first while making minimum payments on other debts. Once that debt is paid off, you move on to the next highest interest rate debt. The debt snowball method, on the other hand, involves paying off the smallest debt first while making minimum payments on other debts. This method provides a psychological boost as you see debts being eliminated quickly, which can motivate you to continue your debt repayment journey.

Subsection 4: Seeking Additional Income

If your current income is not sufficient to cover your debt repayment plan, consider seeking additional sources of income. This could involve taking on a part-time job, freelancing, or selling unused items. The extra income can help expedite your debt repayment process and provide financial relief sooner.

Subsection 5: Staying Motivated

Paying off holiday debt requires discipline and perseverance. To stay motivated, set smaller goals along the way and reward yourself when you achieve them. Celebrate each debt you pay off by treating yourself to a small indulgence or a special experience. Additionally, find support from friends, family, or online communities that share the same financial goals. Surrounding yourself with like-minded individuals can provide encouragement and accountability throughout your debt repayment journey.

Subsection 6: Utilizing Budgeting Tools and Resources

In today's digital age, numerous budgeting tools and resources are available to help you manage your finances effectively. Consider using mobile apps or online platforms that allow you to track your spending, set financial goals, and monitor your progress. These tools can provide valuable insights into your spending habits and help you make informed decisions about your finances.

Subsection 7: Staying Financially Healthy Beyond the Holidays

Avoiding post-holiday debt is not just about paying off your immediate obligations; it's also about developing healthy financial habits that will serve you well throughout the year. As you work toward paying off your holiday debt, take the opportunity to reflect on your spending habits and identify areas where you can make long-term improvements. Consider creating a monthly budget, building an emergency fund, and exploring strategies to save money on a regular basis. By adopting these practices, you can build a strong financial foundation that will protect you from future debt and provide peace of mind.

Conclusion

Post-holiday debt can be a significant burden, but with careful planning and disciplined execution, it is possible to overcome it. By assessing your debt, prioritizing your payments, creating a repayment plan, and utilizing budgeting tools and resources, you can take control of your financial situation and avoid the pitfalls of post-holiday debt. Remember, it's not just about paying off your current obligations; it's about developing healthy financial habits that will benefit you for years to come. Stay motivated, seek support when needed, and celebrate each milestone along the way. With determination and perseverance, you can regain your financial freedom and make the most of your holiday season and beyond.

Mastering Post-Holiday Spending: A Financial Game Plan

The holiday season is a time of joy, celebration, and giving.

However, it's also a time when many people find themselves burdened with post-holiday debt. The allure of sales, promotions, and irresistible deals can make it easy to overspend and lose track of your budget. In this section, we will explore effective strategies and practical tips to help you avoid post-holiday debt and maintain financial stability. Let's dive in!

Subsection 1: Creating a Plan for Paying off Holiday Debt

To start your journey towards a debt-free post-holiday season, it's essential to create a plan for paying off any accumulated debt. Here are some steps to help you get started:

1. Assess Your Current Financial Situation: Begin by reviewing your financial statements, credit card bills, and any outstanding loans. Take note of the total amount of debt you have accumulated during the holiday season. This will give you a clear understanding of where you stand financially.

2. Set Realistic Goals: Determine how much you can afford to pay each month towards your debt. It's important to set realistic goals that align with your income and other financial obligations. Remember, paying off debt is a gradual process, so be patient and persistent.

3. Prioritize Your Debt: If you have multiple debts, prioritize them based on interest rates. Start by paying off high-interest debts first, as they can accumulate more interest over time. Make minimum payments on other debts while focusing on eliminating the high-interest ones.

4. Consider Debt Consolidation: If you have multiple debts with varying interest rates, consider consolidating them into a single loan or credit card with a lower interest rate. Debt consolidation can simplify your payments and potentially save you money on interest.

Subsection 2: Tips for Avoiding Overspending

During Post-Holiday Sales

Post-holiday sales are notorious for tempting shoppers with irresistible discounts and promotions. Here are some tips to help you resist the urge to overspend:

1. Set a Budget: Before diving into post-holiday sales, set a budget for yourself. Determine how much you can afford to spend without going into debt. Stick to this budget and avoid exceeding it, no matter how tempting the deals may be.

2. Make a List: Create a list of items you genuinely need or have been planning to purchase. Focus on these items and avoid impulse buying. Remember, just because an item is on sale doesn't mean you need it or that it's a good deal.

3. Research Prices: Before making a purchase, research prices and compare them across different stores. Don't assume that every post-holiday sale price is the best. Some retailers may offer better deals than others, so take the time to find the best value for your money.

4. Avoid Store Credit Cards: While store credit cards may offer additional discounts during post-holiday sales, be cautious about opening new lines of credit. These cards often come with high-interest rates and can lead to unnecessary debt if not managed carefully.

Subsection 3: Utilizing Budgeting Tools and Resources to Stay on Track

Staying on track with your finances requires discipline and organization. Here are some budgeting tools and resources that can help:

1. Personal Finance Apps: Use personal finance apps like Mint or YNAB (You Need A Budget) to track your expenses, set savings goals, and monitor your progress. These apps provide valuable insights into your spending habits and

can help you make informed financial decisions.

2. Automated Savings: Set up automatic transfers from your checking account to a separate savings account. This ensures that a portion of your income is saved before you have a chance to spend it. Automating your savings makes it easier to stick to your budget and build an emergency fund.

3. Seek Professional Advice: Consider consulting a financial advisor or credit counselor for personalized guidance. These professionals can provide expert advice tailored to your specific financial situation and help you develop a long-term plan for financial success.

By following these strategies and implementing these practical tips, you can avoid post-holiday debt and maintain financial stability. Remember, the true spirit of the holidays lies in creating lasting memories with loved ones and finding joy in alternative gift-giving. With a solid financial game plan in place, you can make this post-holiday season a debt-free and fulfilling one. Happy saving and happy holidays!

Mastering Post-Holiday Debt: Strategies for a Debt-Free New Year

The holiday season is a time of joy, celebration, and giving. However, it can also be a time of financial stress and post-holiday debt. If you're not careful, overspending during the holidays can leave you with a hefty pile of bills to pay off in the new year. But fear not, there are several strategies you can employ to avoid post-holiday debt and start the new year on a financially secure note.

Subsection 1: Creating a Plan for Paying off Holiday Debt

1.1 Assess Your Post-Holiday Financial Situation

Before you can create a plan for paying off your holiday debt, you need to know exactly how much debt you're facing. Take the time to gather all your credit card statements, receipts, and any other relevant financial documents. Add up the total amount you spent during the holiday season and compare it to your available funds. This will give you a clear picture of the debt you need to tackle.

1.2 Prioritize Your Debts

Once you have a clear understanding of your post-holiday debt, it's time to prioritize which debts to pay off first. Start by focusing on high-interest debts, such as credit card balances, as they tend to accrue the most interest over time. Make a list of all your debts, from highest interest rate to lowest interest rate, and allocate a portion of your monthly budget towards paying off these debts.

1.3 Set a Realistic Debt Repayment Plan

To effectively pay off your holiday debt, you need to set a realistic repayment plan. Calculate how much you can comfortably afford to put towards debt repayment each month without compromising your basic living expenses. Set a target date for paying off your debt and break it down into manageable monthly payments. Stick to your plan and make consistent payments to chip away at your debt gradually.

Subsection 2: Tips for Avoiding Overspending During Post-Holiday Sales

2.1 Set a Strict Budget

One of the biggest temptations during post-holiday sales is the lure of discounted prices. However, it's essential to resist the urge to overspend. Before you hit the stores or browse the online sales, set a strict budget for yourself. Determine how much you can afford to spend without going into further debt and stick to that budget rigorously.

2.2 Make a List and Stick to It

To avoid impulse purchases, make a list of the items you genuinely need or have been planning to buy. Whether it's household essentials, clothing items, or electronics, having a list will keep you focused and prevent you from making unnecessary purchases. Cross items off your list as you buy them, and resist the temptation to deviate from it.

2.3 Avoid Emotional Purchases

Post-holiday sales can be enticing, with flashy advertisements and seemingly unbeatable deals. However, it's crucial to approach these sales with a rational mindset. Avoid making emotional purchases based on impulse or FOMO (fear of missing out). Take the time to research products, compare prices, and consider whether the purchase aligns with your financial goals and priorities.

Subsection 3: Utilizing Budgeting Tools and Resources to Stay on Track

3.1 Track Your Expenses

One of the most effective ways to avoid post-holiday debt is by tracking your expenses. Use budgeting tools and resources such as mobile apps, spreadsheets, or online platforms to monitor your spending. Categorize your expenses and analyze where your money is going. This will help you identify areas where you can cut back and make adjustments to stay within your budget.

3.2 Use Cash Envelopes

If you find it challenging to stick to your budget, consider using the cash envelope system. Allocate a specific amount of cash to different spending categories, such as groceries, entertainment, or clothing. Place the cash in separate envelopes labeled with the category name. Once the money in the envelope is gone, you can no longer spend in that category until the next budgeting period. This method adds a tangible element to budgeting and helps you visually see how much money you have left in each category.

3.3 Seek Professional Financial Advice

If you're struggling to manage your post-holiday debt or need guidance on budgeting and financial planning, don't hesitate to seek professional advice. Consult a financial advisor or credit counselor who can provide personalized strategies to help you get back on track. They can offer insights on debt consolidation, negotiating lower interest rates, or creating a long-term financial plan.

By following these strategies, you can avoid post-holiday debt and start the new year on a financially sound footing. Remember, it's not just about the joy of giving during the holiday season, but also about giving yourself the gift of financial peace of mind. Take control of your finances, set realistic goals, and make informed spending decisions to ensure a debt-free and prosperous new year.

Avoiding Post-Holiday Debt: Key Takeaways

As we conclude this chapter on avoiding post-holiday debt, let's recap the key points and provide you with actionable advice to help you stay on track and enjoy a debt-free start to the new year.

Creating a plan for paying off holiday debt is crucial. Take the time to assess your financial situation, set achievable goals, and develop a repayment strategy that works for you. Remember, small steps in the right direction can lead to significant progress.

When it comes to post-holiday sales, it's important to resist the temptation to overspend. Keep your budget in mind and stay focused on purchasing only what you need. By avoiding impulsive buying and sticking to your list, you can prevent unnecessary debt and regret.

Utilizing budgeting tools and resources can be a game-changer. From smartphone apps to spreadsheets, there are various tools available to help you track your expenses, set budgets, and monitor your progress. Find what works best for you and make it a part of your financial routine.

In closing, remember that the true spirit of the holiday season lies in creating memories and cherishing time with loved ones, not in accumulating debt. By following the tips outlined in this chapter, you can ensure a financially responsible and stress-free start to the new year. Make smart choices, prioritize your financial well-being, and enjoy the holiday season without the burden of post-holiday debt.

CHAPTER 10 : EMBRACING THE TRUE SPIRIT OF THE HOLIDAYS

Welcome to Chapter 10 of 'Spend Less and Get More: Your Ultimate Holiday Guide.' In this chapter, we will delve deep into the heart of the holiday season, exploring the true spirit that lies beneath the hustle and bustle of the festivities. It is a time to pause, reflect, and reconnect with what truly matters. As we navigate through the holiday season, it is easy to get caught up in the whirlwind of shopping lists, party planning, and financial stress.

But in this chapter, we invite you to step back from the chaos and rediscover the joy and meaning that the holidays can bring. The true spirit of the holidays is not found in the material possessions or the extravagant displays. It resides in the intangible moments that touch our hearts and create lasting memories. It is about gratitude, giving back, and finding joy in the simplest of pleasures.

Finding Joy in the Simple Pleasures of the Season

The holiday season is often associated with grand gestures,

extravagant gifts, and elaborate decorations. However, true joy can often be found in the simplest of pleasures. In this section, we will explore how to embrace the true spirit of the holidays by focusing on the small moments and simple joys that make this time of year truly special.

Subsection 1: Savoring the Magic of Winter

The arrival of winter brings with it a sense of magic and wonder. Instead of rushing through the season, take the time to slow down and savor the beauty of winter. Bundle up and take a walk in the snow, marvel at the glistening icicles hanging from trees, or simply sit by a cozy fire with a warm cup of cocoa. These simple activities can help you appreciate the beauty and tranquility of the season.

Subsection 2: Embracing the Power of Traditions

Traditions play a significant role in creating lasting memories and a sense of belonging. Whether it's decorating the Christmas tree, baking holiday cookies, or singing carols with loved ones, traditions connect us to our past and bring a sense of comfort and joy. Take the time to reflect on the traditions that hold meaning for you and your family, and make an effort to continue or create new traditions that can be passed down through generations.

Subsection 3: Cultivating Gratitude

The holiday season is the perfect time to cultivate an attitude of gratitude. It's easy to get caught up in the hustle and bustle of shopping and party planning, but taking a moment each day to reflect on the things you are grateful for can bring a sense of peace and contentment. Keep a gratitude journal, write thank-you notes, or simply take a few minutes each day to silently express gratitude for the people and experiences that enrich your life.

Subsection 4: Giving from the Heart

One of the most rewarding aspects of the holiday season

is the act of giving. While it's easy to get caught up in the commercialism of the holidays, the true joy comes from giving from the heart. Consider volunteering your time at a local charity, donating to a cause you're passionate about, or finding small ways to make a difference in the lives of others. The act of giving not only benefits those in need but also brings a sense of fulfillment and purpose to your own life.

Subsection 5: Embracing Simplicity

In a world that is often filled with excess and consumerism, embracing simplicity can be a refreshing change of pace. Instead of getting caught up in the pressure to buy extravagant gifts or host elaborate parties, focus on the simple joys that the holiday season has to offer. Spend quality time with loved ones, engage in meaningful conversations, and create memories that will last a lifetime. Remember, it's not about the size or cost of the gifts but the love and thought behind them.

By finding joy in the simple pleasures of the season, you can truly embrace the true spirit of the holidays. Take the time to savor the magic of winter, embrace traditions, cultivate gratitude, give from the heart, and embrace simplicity. These small but meaningful actions will not only make your holiday season more joyful but also create lasting memories that will warm your heart for years to come.

Finding Joy in the Simple Pleasures of the Season

The holiday season is often associated with extravagant gifts, lavish parties, and extravagant decorations. However, it's important to remember that the true spirit of the holidays lies in finding joy in the simple pleasures that money can't buy. In this section, we will explore some of the ways you can embrace the true essence of the holidays and create lasting memories without breaking the bank.

Subsection 1: Embracing the Joy of Giving

One of the most fulfilling aspects of the holidays is the act of giving. While it's tempting to get caught up in the consumerism of the season, finding joy in giving does not have to come with a hefty price tag. Consider these ideas:

1. Volunteer your time: Giving your time to those in need is a meaningful way to make a difference. Whether it's serving meals at a local shelter or spending time with the elderly at a nursing home, your presence can bring immeasurable joy to others.

2. Make homemade gifts: Instead of spending a fortune on store-bought presents, consider making personalized gifts from the heart. Whether it's a batch of homemade cookies, a hand-knitted scarf, or a heartfelt letter, these gifts will be cherished for their thoughtfulness and effort.

3. Donate to charity: Instead of exchanging gifts with friends and family, consider pooling your resources and making a donation to a charitable cause. Not only will you be making a positive impact on the lives of others, but you'll also create a sense of unity and purpose among your loved ones.

Subsection 2: Creating Meaningful Traditions

Traditions play a significant role in the holiday season, as they provide a sense of continuity and connection with the past. Here are some ideas for creating meaningful traditions that can be enjoyed year after year:

1. Family movie night: Pick a holiday classic that holds special meaning for your family and make it a tradition to watch it together every year. Pop some popcorn, cuddle up on the couch, and enjoy the warmth and nostalgia that comes with sharing a beloved film.

2. Advent calendar activities: Instead of purchasing a store-

bought advent calendar filled with chocolates or toys, create your own with daily activities that foster togetherness. Each day, open a new window and discover a fun activity to do as a family, such as baking cookies, going for a winter hike, or playing board games.

3. Giving back as a family: Instill a sense of gratitude and generosity in your children by involving them in acts of kindness. Whether it's volunteering at a local food bank or organizing a toy drive for underprivileged children, these experiences will teach them the value of giving back and create cherished memories.

Subsection 3: Finding Joy in Nature

The holiday season is a perfect time to reconnect with nature and find joy in its simple beauty. Here are a few ways to incorporate nature into your holiday celebrations:

1. Take a winter nature walk: Bundle up and explore the outdoors with a brisk winter walk. Notice the beauty of bare trees, the crunch of snow beneath your feet, and the crispness of the air. This simple activity can bring a sense of peace and tranquility amidst the chaos of the season.

2. Decorate with natural elements: Instead of purchasing expensive decorations, consider bringing the beauty of nature indoors. Use pinecones, branches, and holly berries to create festive centerpieces and wreaths. Not only will these decorations be visually appealing, but they will also fill your home with the fresh scent of nature.

3. Enjoy a bonfire or campfire: Gather your loved ones and cozy up around a warm fire. Roast marshmallows, tell stories, and revel in the simple pleasure of spending time together in the great outdoors.

By focusing on gratitude, giving back, creating meaningful traditions, and finding joy in the simple pleasures of the season, you can truly embrace the true spirit of the holidays. Remember, it's not about how much you spend or how extravagant your celebrations are, but rather the love, joy, and connection that you share with your loved ones. This holiday season, let's make an effort to slow down, appreciate the little things, and create lasting memories that will warm our hearts for years to come.

Conclusion

As we come to the end of 'Spend Less and Get More: Your Ultimate Holiday Guide,' it is time to reflect on the wealth of knowledge and strategies we have explored together. Throughout this book, we have journeyed through the intricacies of holiday expenses and discovered the power of embracing a frugal mindset. Now, armed with actionable advice, it is time for you to unleash your holiday magic and create a joyful and thrifty celebration. Let's recap the key points that we have covered:

 - Creating a holiday budget: We learned the importance of setting realistic financial boundaries and allocating funds to different aspects of the holiday season. By creating a budget, you can take control of your expenses and make informed decisions.

 - Smart shopping strategies: We explored the art of strategic shopping, from making lists and comparing prices to taking advantage of sales and discounts. With these tactics, you can stretch your dollar further and find the best deals.

 - DIY gifts and decorations: We discovered the joy of creating personalized gifts and decorations. By tapping into your creativity, you can add a heartfelt touch to your celebrations while saving money.

 - Maximizing savings: We delved into various ways to maximize your savings, such as using coupons, cashback programs, and loyalty rewards. These small steps can add up to significant savings over time.

 - Alternative gift-giving: We embraced the idea of meaningful and experiential gifts that foster deeper connections with our loved ones. By focusing on shared experiences rather than material possessions, we can create lasting memories.

- Managing holiday travel expenses: We discussed strategies for saving on holiday travel, including booking flights in advance, comparing prices, and considering alternative transportation options. These tips can help you enjoy your journey without breaking the bank.

- Hosting on a budget: We explored ways to host memorable gatherings without overspending. From potluck-style meals to DIY decorations, you can create a warm and inviting atmosphere while keeping costs in check.

- Avoiding post-holiday debt: We emphasized the importance of planning for the aftermath of the holiday season. By being mindful of your spending and avoiding unnecessary debt, you can start the new year on a financially stable note.

- Embracing the true spirit of the holidays: Finally, we discussed the significance of embracing the true essence of the holidays. It's about cherishing the moments spent with loved ones, practicing gratitude, and finding joy in the simple pleasures of the season. Now, armed with these key takeaways, it's time to take action.

Here are some actionable steps you can implement immediately to make the most of the information provided in this book:

1. Create a holiday budget: Sit down and allocate funds for different aspects of the holiday season, ensuring that you stay within your means.

2. Prioritize smart shopping: Make a shopping list, compare prices, and take advantage of sales and discounts to get the best value for your money.

3. Incorporate DIY: Get creative and make personalized gifts and decorations that will add a special touch to your celebrations without breaking the bank.

4. Maximize your savings: Use coupons, cashback programs, and loyalty rewards to save money on your holiday purchases.

5. Explore alternative gift-giving: Consider experiential gifts or shared activities that will create lasting memories with your loved ones.

6. Be mindful of travel expenses: Plan your holiday travel in advance, compare prices, and explore alternative transportation options to save on costs.

7. Host on a budget: Opt for potluck-style gatherings, DIY decorations, and affordable entertainment options to create meaningful experiences without overspending.

8. Avoid post-holiday debt: Practice mindful spending and avoid unnecessary debt by sticking to your budget and prioritizing your financial well-being.

9. Embrace the true spirit of the holidays: Focus on the joy of spending time with loved ones, practicing gratitude, and finding happiness in the little things.

By implementing these steps, you can transform your holiday season into a joyous and budget-friendly experience. Remember, it's not about how much money you spend; it's about the memories you create and the love you share. As we bid farewell, we hope that 'Spend Less and Get More: Your Ultimate Holiday Guide' has provided you with the tools, inspiration, and confidence to make this holiday season truly magical. Embrace the journey, unleash your holiday magic, and create a celebration that reflects your values and brings joy to your heart. Happy holidays!

AFTERWORD

As we close the chapter on "Spend Less and Get More: Holiday Guide," take a moment to reflect on the joyous celebrations you've crafted on a budget. The beauty of frugality lies not just in the savings but in the intentionality of every choice.

May the tips and tricks shared by Olivia Frugal continue to inspire budget-friendly celebrations, reminding us all that the true magic of the holidays is found in the warmth of connection and the joy of shared experiences. Whether you're a seasoned frugal celebrator or a newcomer to the art, this afterword is a nod to the countless celebrations yet to come—each one a testament to the magic that happens when we choose to spend wisely and savor every moment.

With heartfelt wishes for many more joyous and budget-friendly holidays.

ABOUT THE AUTHOR

Olivia Frugal

Meet Olivia Frugal, the anonymous maven behind the "Spend Less and Get More: Holiday Guide." An expert in the art of festive frugality, Olivia's proven tips and budget-friendly strategies promise to transform your holidays without compromising joy. Despite her undisclosed identity, Olivia's dedication to helping you celebrate on a budget shines through, making this guide your go-to resource for memorable, wallet-friendly holidays.

www.ingramcontent.com/pod-product-compliance
Lightning Source LLC
Chambersburg PA
CBHW062237290526
45794CB00006B/2327